I0484635

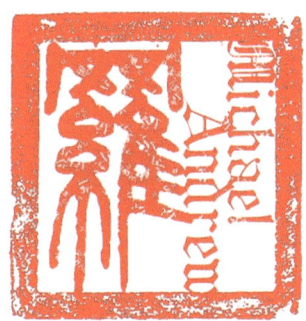

*Cast drawing study*
*Pencil on French Drawing Paper*
*2004*
*59.4 x 84.1cm*
*(international paper size A1)*
*private collection*

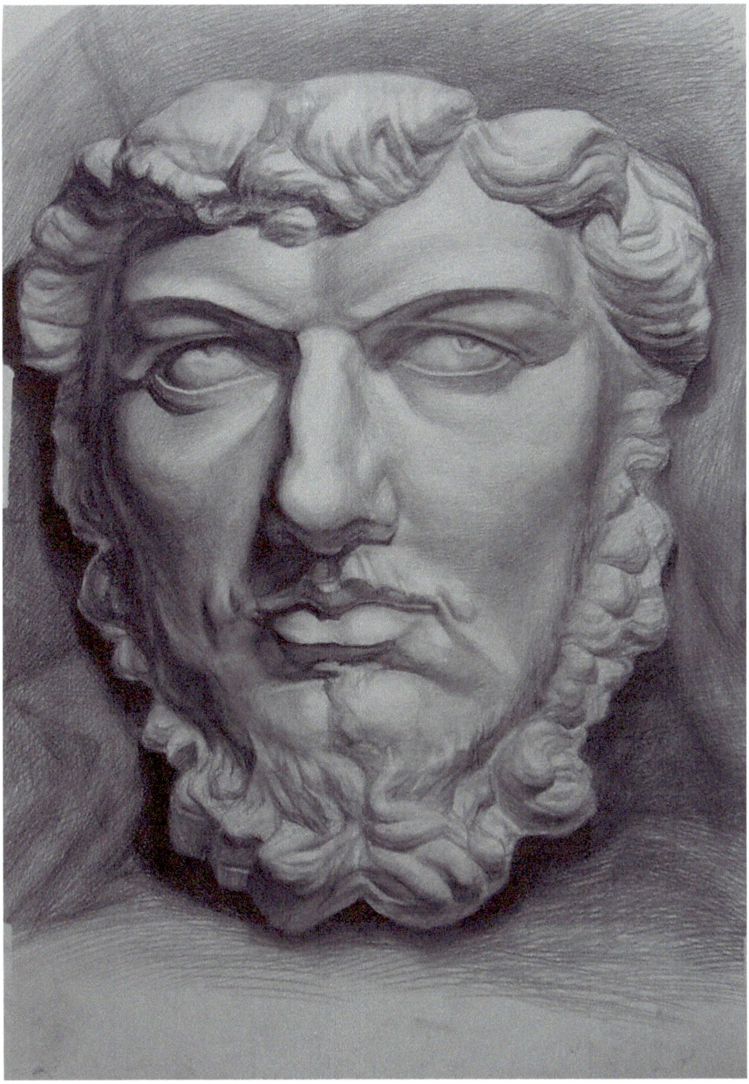

*Cast drawing study*
*Pencil on French Drawing Paper*
*2004*
*59.4 x 84.1cm*
*(international paper size A1)*
*private collection*

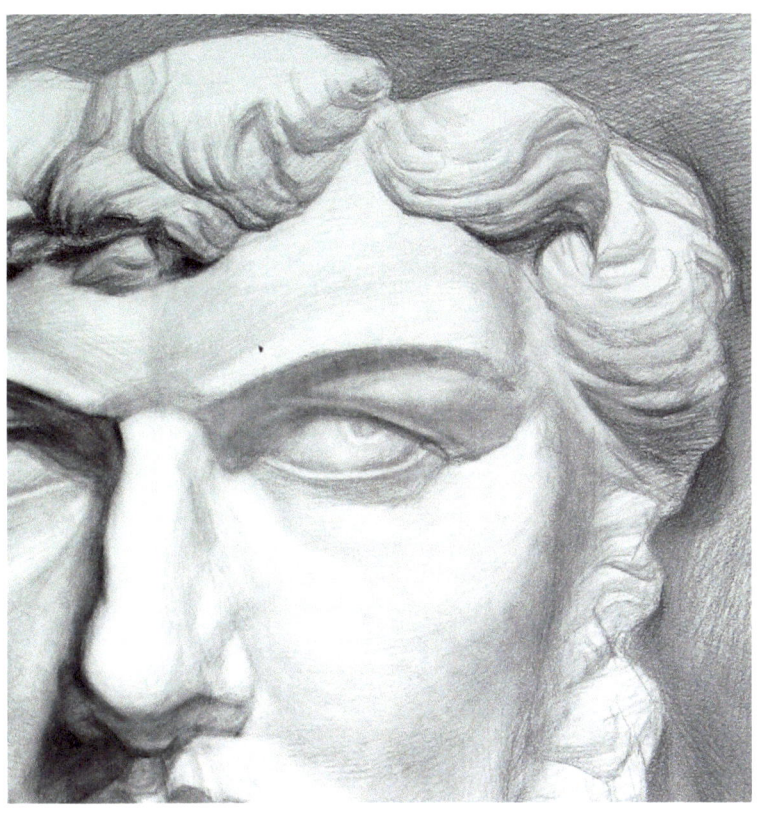

*Cast drawing study*
*Pencil on French Drawing Paper*
*2004*
*59.4 x 84.1cm*
*(international paper size A1)*
*private collection*

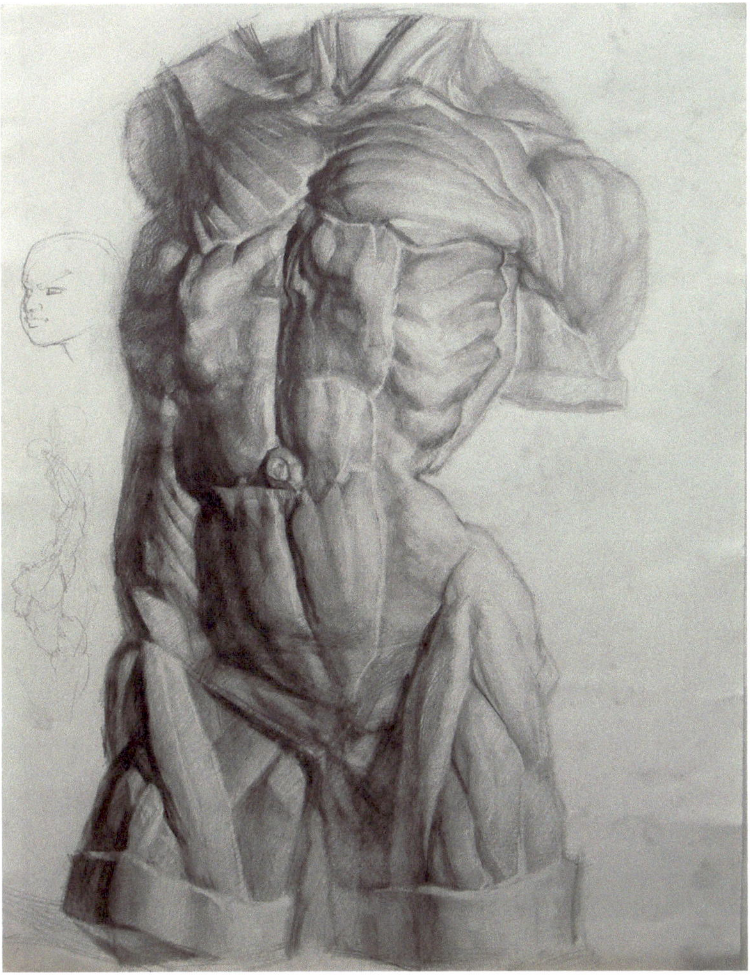

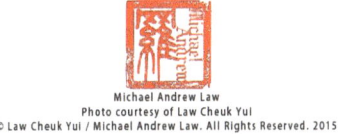

*Cast drawing study*
*Pencil on French Drawing Paper*
*2004*
*59.4 x 84.1cm*
*(international paper size A1)*
*private collection*

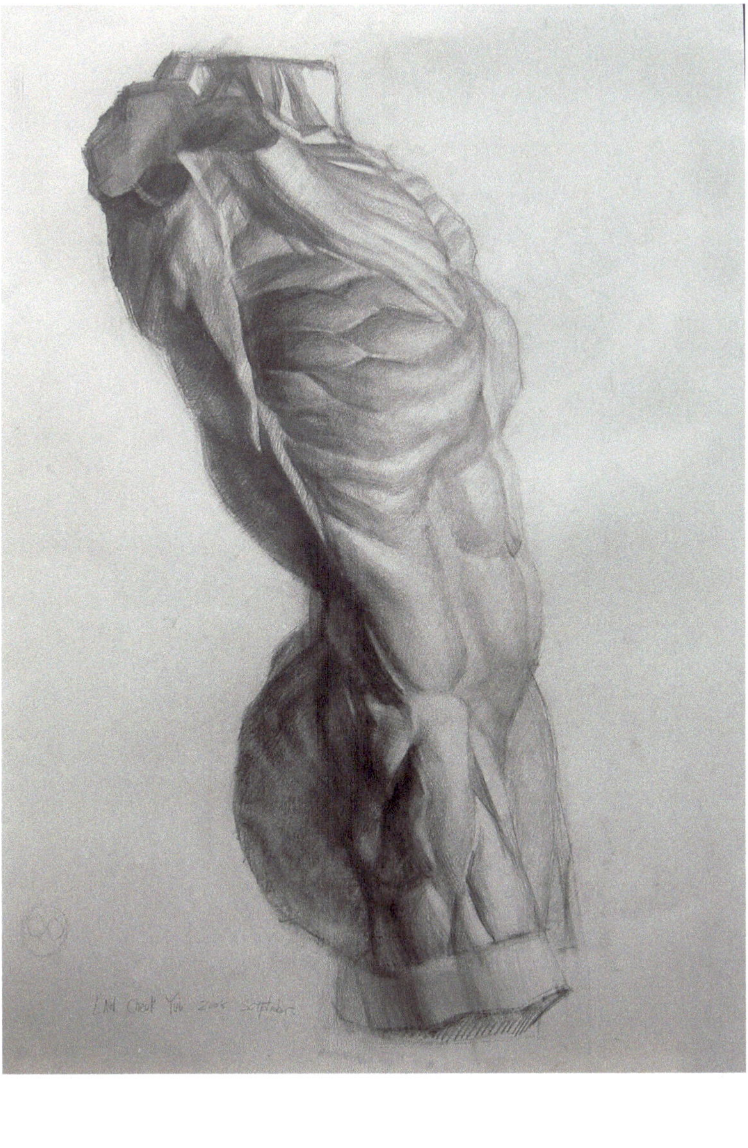

*Cast drawing study*
*Pencil on French Drawing Paper*
*2004*
*59.4 x 84.1cm*
*(international paper size A1)*
*private collection*

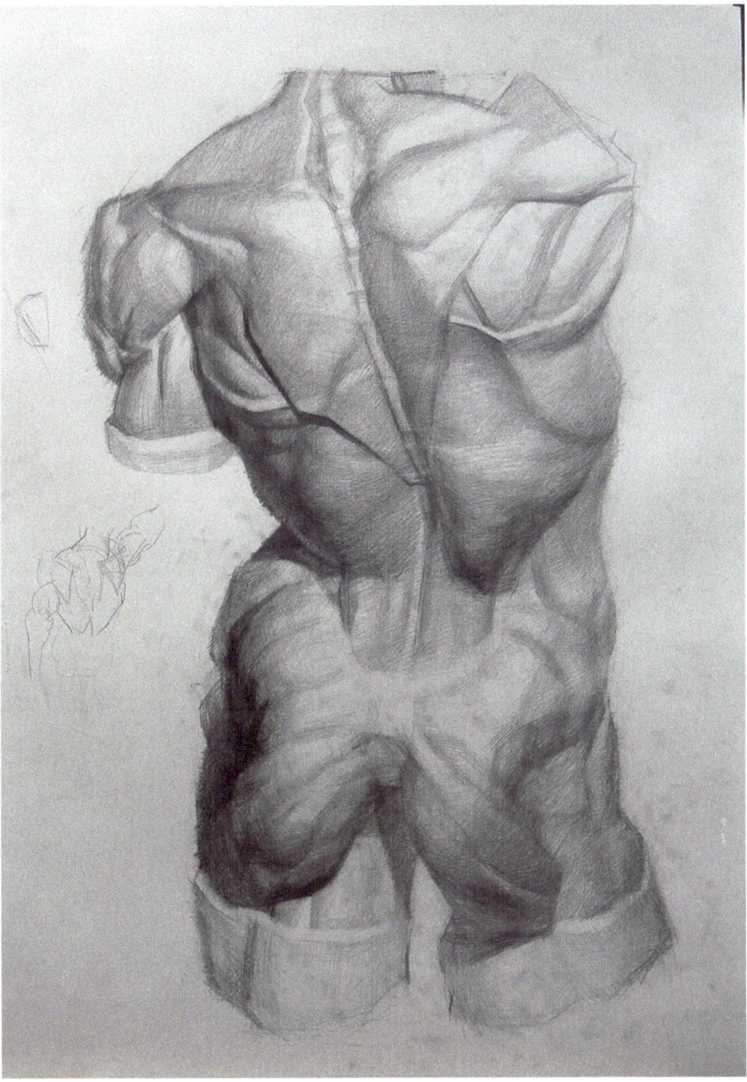

*Cast drawing study*
*Pencil on French Drawing Paper*
*2004*
*59.4 x 84.1cm*
*(international paper size A1)*
*private collection*

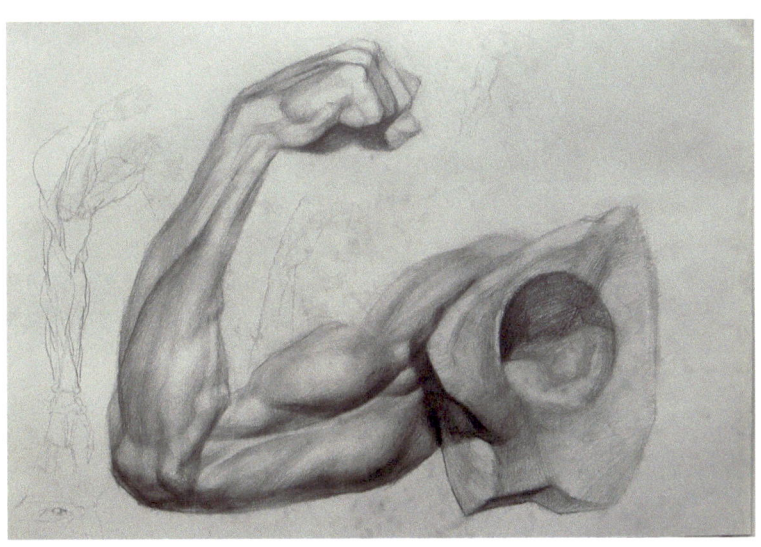

Cast drawing study
Pencil on French Drawing Paper
2004
59.4 x 84.1cm
(international paper size A1)
private collection

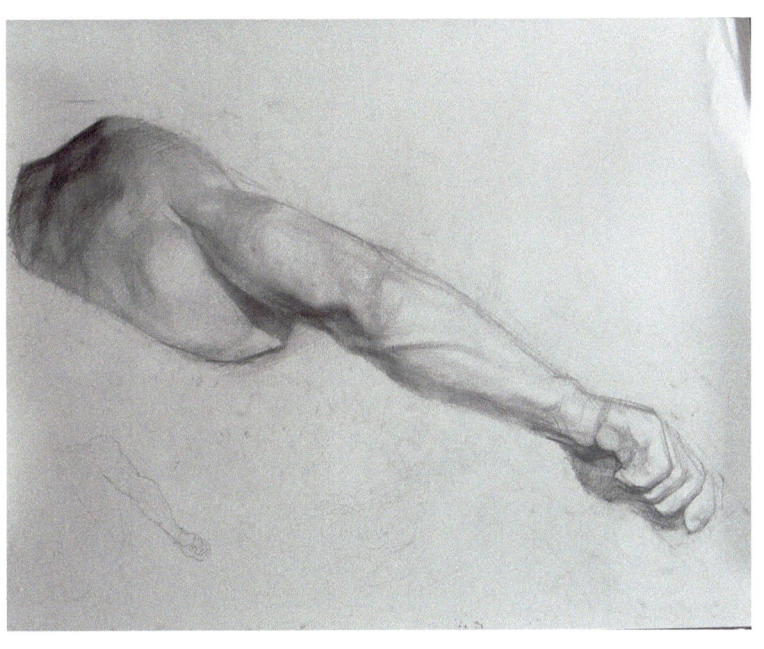

*Cast drawing study*
*Pencil on French Drawing Paper*
*2004*
*59.4 x 84.1cm*
*(international paper size A1)*
*private collection*

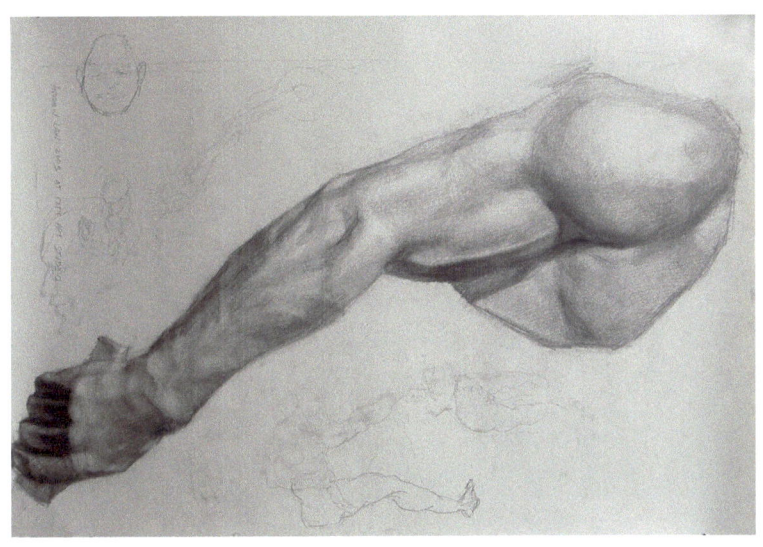

*Cast drawing study*
*Pencil on French Drawing Paper*
*2004*
*59.4 x 84.1cm*
*(international paper size A1)*
*private collection*

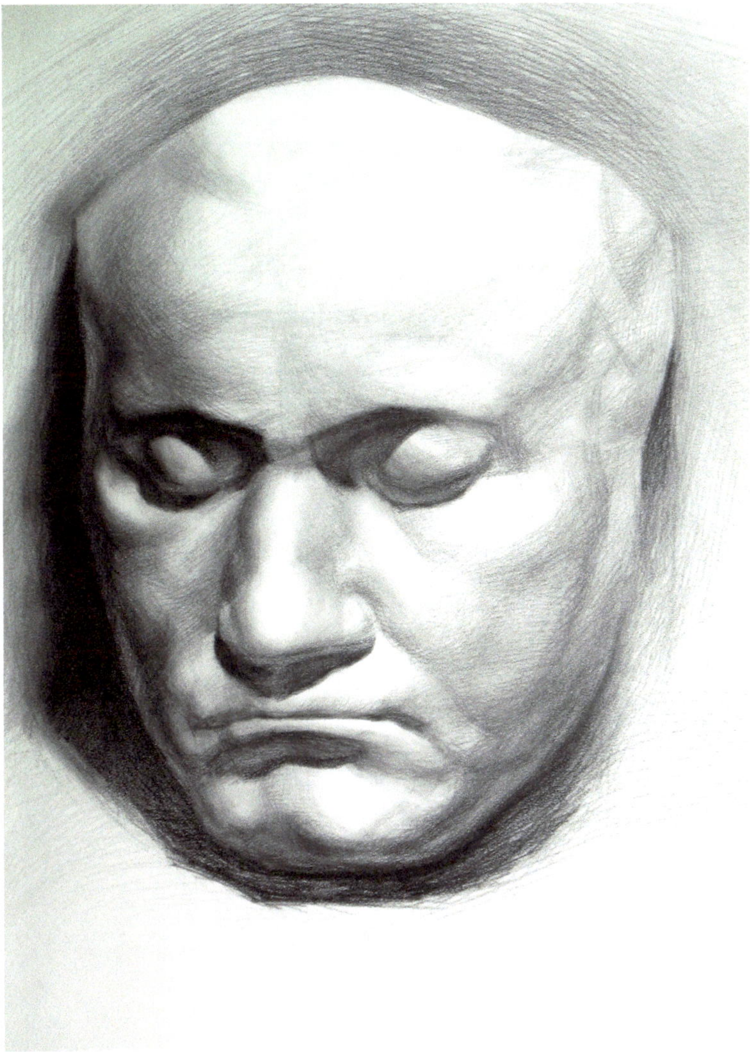

*Cast drawing study*
*Pencil on French Drawing Paper*
*2004*
*59.4 x 84.1cm*
*(international paper size A1)*
*private collection*

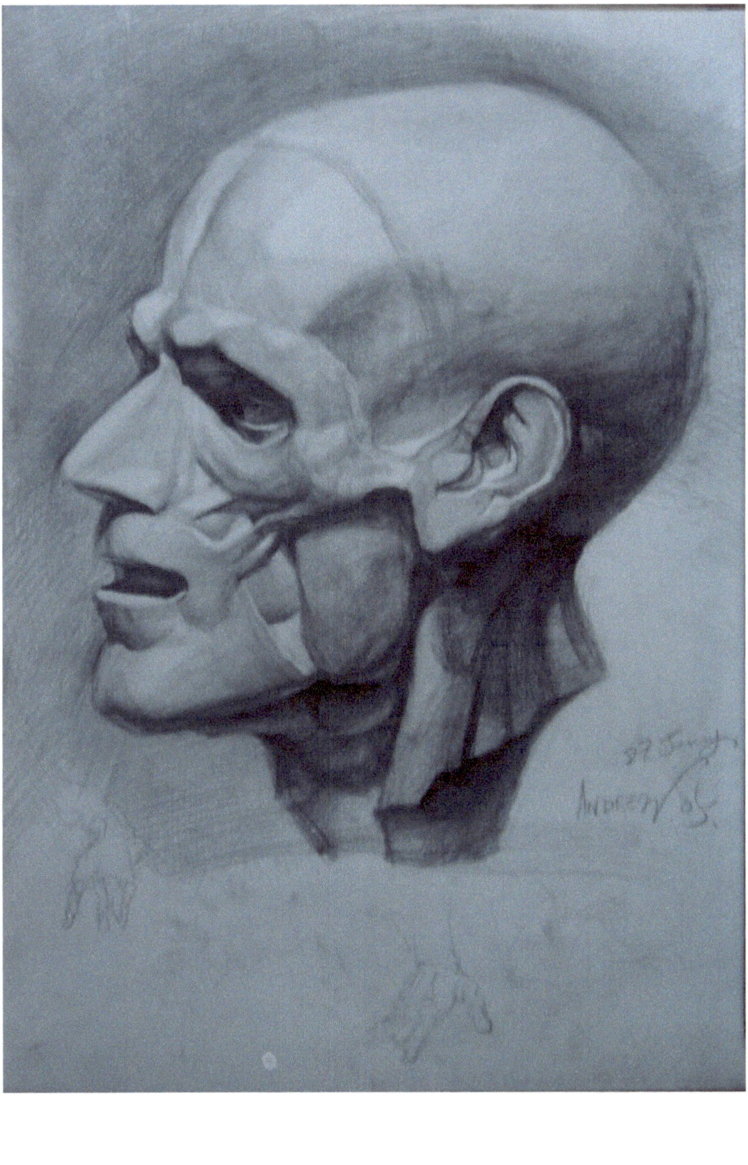

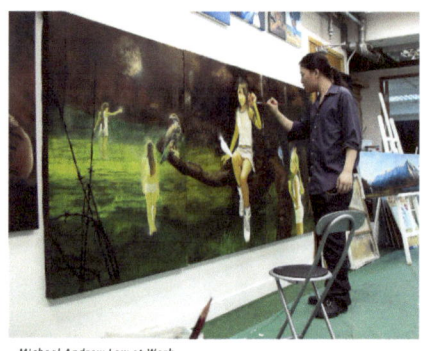

*Michael Andrew Law at Work.*

Michael Andrew Law fusing digital and classical painting with west and East creative philosophy , to produce an extremely original artistic language and content that bridged west and east ,classical and modern medium , at the same time clearly tells the stories of his own generation. Combining digital creative materials and classical painting techniques with effusive yet knowing and precise focused , his paintings maintain a powerful tension between opposing aesthetic forces—expression and knowledge, control and spontaneity, savagery and wit, urbanity and primitivism—while providing satiric commentary on the oppressive realities of the predicament of Generation Internet, homegrown hongkonger's local-culture vesus Traditional Chinese culture, and The Hong Kong's post-handover history.

In his dynamically designed compositions, gracefully detailed figures and innocent faces are incise against fields that juxtaposed  with portraits, chinese calligraphy, and sometimes cgi. The Pale Hair Girls Series (2006 - 2013)  depicts realistic cold, icy-like young female figures surrounded by abstract and expressively painted forms and shapes revealing images of Pop culture, Historial figures, and Hong Kong landmarks.

Michael Andrew Law draws inspiration from Old Master's works such as Caravaggio , Ruben , Rembrandt , all the way to the Modern Art Superstars such as Warhol , Lichtenstein , Richter , De Kooning , Bacon , Wool and Prince . The Pale Hair Girls series mainly  inspired by the painting works of French academic painter and traditionalist William-Adolphe Bouguereau and the Late Great YiFei Chen's characteristic "Romantic Realism" paintings.

In a reversal of standard East-West aesthetics, Law re-interprets Old Master's sophisticated imagery combine classical and digital materials—which resonate with Digital Vector Designs and Paintings—with fine strokes of oil paint multi-layered with paint film.In his interpretation of Leonardo Da Vinci's iconic Mona Lisa's smile (1517)—an iconic image that has been endlessly disseminated and reproduced—Law painted over the symbolism of the portrait Mona Lisa with his young wife , intent on rendering the figure in contemporary fashion with the iconic image as background .

"The Humanity triptych" depicts New Generation HongKongers in a Ruined Hong Kong city , awaiting their unknown fate of a new beginning. This painting series explores one of the central paradox of his art—between romance and derision , his romantic magnanimity as an artist and his pessimistic perspective on the predicament of Generation Y Hongkongers. Here, this paradox is symbolized by the stark contrast of icy cold young female and disturbing representations of the armageddon-like of images. Whether portrayed as single "chinese calligraphy " or in  triptych composition and classical paintwork that combine both expressive and traditional painting techniques with the digital vector , the beauties and the human figures stand as eternal motifs in the history of art and also in popular culture. Both oppositional and parallel, they are reminders of the fragile vibrancy of life and the impitoyable passing of time.

A references between different cultural refrence (high/pop, classical/contemporary, east/west), Michael Andrew Law has stated that an artist should be someone who understood how to hybrid between different worlds and go ahead makes an effort to knowing them. With his distinctive "iEgoism" philosophy , which employs highly refined academic painting techniques to depict a mixture of abstract expressionism within a representational pop culture images. These techniques parallel to the themes of romance and predicament of this generation , he recollects and revitalizes narratives of irony and introspection.

Michael Andrew Lawwas born in 1982 in British Hong
Kong , studied fine art with american artist Daniel
Anderson and graduate of China Central Academy of
Fine Arts Sam Zeng from 2003 - 2006 . He co-founded
the Hong Kong Art Studio Nature Art Workshop in
2008. In addition to the production and marketing of
Michael Andrew Law's art and related work, Nature Art
functions as a supportive environment for the
fostering of emerging Hong Konger artists. Law is also
a curator. In 2013, he organized an exhibition of
contemporary art titled "iEgoism ," which served as
a commentaries of contemporary HongKong Gen Y pop
culture ;These Theroy also published in the book :
"iEgoism" in 2014.

Michael Andrew Law currently works and lives in Hong
Kong.

For further information please contact the studio at
info@michaelandrewlaw.com or at +852.6444.7550. All
images are subject to copyright. Artist/Studio/Gallery's
approval must be granted prior to reproduction.

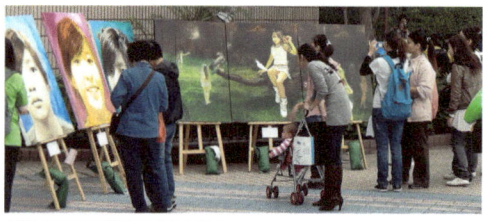

*2010 Avenue of Stars, Hong Kong*

Exhibition :

2013 DeTour Matters 2013 Satellite Events at NatureArt Gallery
2013 December to Remember , One man show at NatureArt Gallery Central District, Hong Kong.
2012 Solo Show , Park Central tseung kwan O ,Hong Kong
2011 Art Walk Group Showing , Discovery Bay ,Hong Kong
2011 HK Gold Coast (Book signing exhibition)
2009 Solo Painting Exhibition The Avenue of Stars
Group Exhibition of Daniel Anderson workshop Classical Realism class of 2008 at Manhattan,NY
2007 Guest and ExhibitionThe Peak Galleria Hong Kong
2007 invited workshop exhibition, Elements, Hong Kong
Group Exhibition of Classical Realism class of 2007 at Manhattan,NY
2006 Collection by Cardinal Zen Ze-kiun and exhibited at Catholic Church of Hong Kong.
2004 - 2007, Hong Kong Young Artist Group Exhibition, Hong Kong Central Library.
Group Exhibition of Classical Realism class of 2006 at East Village, Manhattan,NY
2005 Illustration original exhibition for Kung Kao Po
2004 Group Exhibition, Wanchai Tower
2003 Group Exhibition, Hong Kong Convention and Exhibition Centre,
2003 Winner of I luv Hong Kong Painting Competition, exhibition at The Landmark (Hong Kong).
2002 The Holy story Picture Book illustrated picture original exhibition ,sai wan ho civic centre.

SELECTED COLLECTIONS :

Cardinal of the Catholic Church Joseph Zen Ze-kiun
Organic Beauty Inc
Agriculture, Fisheries and Conservation Department
Ms.Ho Wei Ying
Ms. Annie Yu
Daniel Anderson
MR.Tsang Yan Sam

PUBLICATIONS :

Fisheye magazine , featured artist interview , November 2002
Kung Kao Po , interview , June 2006
Art of Rock Realism , 2008
The Art of Michael Andrew Law , 2010
December to Remember One man Show Art Book, 2013
iEgoism , 2015

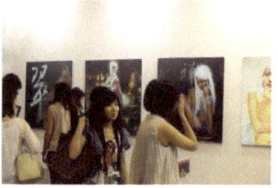

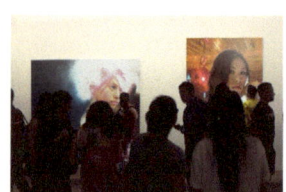

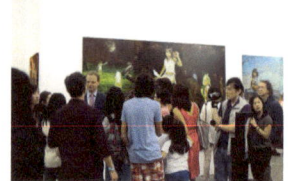

*Solo Shows 2010 - 2013*